SELECTED POEMS

BRENDAN KENNELLY
SELECTED POEMS

E. P. DUTTON & CO. INC.,
NEW YORK 1972

First published in the U.S.A. 1971 by E. P. Dutton & Co., Inc.

©Allen Figgis & Co. Ltd., Dublin and Brendan Kennelly1969
All rights reserved.

Made and Printed in the Republic of Ireland by Cahill & Co.
Limited, Dublin.

First Edition: Dublin 1969.
2nd Edition, Enlarged: New York 1971.

Published simultaneously in Canada by Clarke, Irwin &
Company Limited, Toronto and Vancouver.

Library of Congress Catalog Card Number : 79-177251

SBN 0-525-04425-6

CONTENTS

PREFACE

THERE are many ways in which I might arrange a selection of my poems. The straight chronological order is perhaps the most obvious; on reflection, it also appears the most honest and effective. The first purpose of any selection is to illustrate a poet's growth; and growth can happen only as time passes. The truest reflection of growth, therefore, is the time-pattern, the simple, inevitable day-to-day and year-to-year pattern of living, thinking, feeling, imagining and writing. Anything else is merely clever distortion—a coy, spurious manipulation of poems that pretends to categorize the products of the imagination but in fact falsifies its processes. May I comment briefly then on the three books of poems I have published since 1966 and on my selection from them.

My poems seem to fall naturally into three divisions: poems about the countryside; poems about the city; and poems which, broadly speaking, make an attempt to express some kind of personal philosophy or try to define the nature of personal vision. Let me say immediately that any division of poems is arbitrary and can be easily disproved. What matters is vision and the uniqueness of vision. For example, the way I see a pig-killer at work or the way in which I try to understand history is not separable, essentially, from the way I see scraps of paper in a city street late at night or how I try to understand ideas of, say, goodness and treachery, Judas's relationship with

Christ, a badger killing a hound, the meaning of a quick gesture, or the significance hidden behind words spoken in jest. At the same time, when categories become apparent, it may be helpful to point them out. In my case the causes are simple. I was born in Kerry and lived there for nearly twenty years. I have been living in and out of Dublin for about twelve years and have spent a fair amount of that time studying and teaching in universities. Hence the three divisions I've mentioned. They don't really matter. I merely point them out.

What matters, as I've said before, is vision and the ever-asked, ever-unanswered question involved with it: what is poetry? There have been many attempts to define it. Ultimately, each poet must define it for himself. I find it impossible to define, fascinating to describe. I see it basically as a celebration of human inadequacy and failure. I know that in the deepest sense poetry educates the poet: it leads him through confusion into clarity and simplicity. It teaches the poet about himself, telling him about things in himself such as dedication and hypocrisy. It leads him into severe definitions. It outlaws vagueness. Because it wants to be pure, purely itself, not concerned with deceiving or flattering or making an impact, it towers above him like a judge who, hearing the poet's case over and over, and appraising it constantly and with total fair-mindedness, is incapable of giving a wrong judgement. Poets may deceive; poetry cannot.

I hope I don't seem pretentious in discussing the nature of vision but to me it is all-important. In a poem called "The Blind Man" I try to say what I mean. I believe that each of us is blind in a great number of ways; and that saves us. I believe that occasionally we see things in our blindness; and that elevates us. We are cripplingly limited. To recognize this is a strength. To celebrate it is to discover a kind of indestructibility, to achieve definition, to be purified by the poem:

> . . . vision is not simply seeing straight
> And things discoverable without exist within.
> My shells and birds are different yet elate
> Me utterly. Images that spin
> Within these limits are my own
> With colours, shapes and forms that I create,
> Discovered somewhere in the blood and bone—
> I only see whatever I can make.

The poet and the man blind-from-birth are one in this: the real world is the made world, the world that is achieved through the image.

Vision is an attempt to make sense out of the world. I mean that, quite literally, poetry makes order out of chaos. It unites elements which seem incapable of unity. It detects and reveals coherent pattern in what appears meaningless and accidental. At least it does this for me, and this creation of unity I take to be one of its primary functions. May I take one example of this.

In "My Dark Fathers" (*Collection One*) I tried to define my own relationship with Irish history. One day I attended a talk given by Frank O'Connor about the famine that happened in Ireland in the nineteenth century and had such harrowing effects on the Irish character. I was trying, at the time, to write a poem about that history which I had lived with since childhood. During his talk, O'Connor spoke of a traveller's (Mrs. Asenoth Nicholson's) description of a woman dancing on the Kerry shore:

> This woman, who danced before me, was more than fifty, and I do not believe that the daughter of Herodias herself was more graceful in her movements, more beautiful in her complexion or symmetry, than was this dark-haired matron of the mountains of Kerry.

This image struck me immediately. The woman was the entire people, capable of spontaneous artistic expression; capable of it, that is, before the famine. But then came the terrible desolation. O'Connor made me aware of Peadar O Laoghaire's *Mo Sgéal Féin* where there is the following description of the dead and dying:

> You saw them there every morning after the night out, stretched in rows, some moving and some very still, with no stir from them. Later people came and lifted those who no longer moved and heaved them into carts and carried them up to a place near Carrigastyra, where a big deep pit was open for them, and thrust them into the pit.

This is "the pit of doom" in my poem. There is a description of a man named Paddy bringing his wife Kate from the workhouse back to his hut:

> Next day a neighbour came to the hut. He saw the two of them dead and his wife's feet clasped in Paddy's bosom as though he were trying to warm them. It would seem that he felt the death agony come on Kate and her legs grow cold, so he put them inside his own shirt to take the chill from them.

In the poem I identify this woman, dead from famine disease, her "perished feet nailed to her man's breastbone," with the woman comparable to the daughter of Herodias, dancing on the shore in Kerry. Perhaps the most frightening consequence of famine is described in George Petrie's collection of *The Ancient Music of Ireland*—the terrible, unbearable silence. To my mind, this meant not only the silence that followed racial suffering akin to what Hitler inflicted on the Jews, but it meant that Ireland became the grave of song. I was witnessing the death of the dance:

> This awful, unwonted silence which, during the famine and subsequent years, almost everywhere prevailed, struck more fearfully upon their imaginations, as many Irish gentlemen informed me, and gave them a deeper feeling of the desolation with which the country had been visited, than any other circumstance which had forced itself upon their attention.†

These images of the pit, the woman, the rows of dead, the terrible silence, were in my mind after hearing O'Connor talk. Shortly afterwards, I was at a wedding and a boy was asked to sing. He did so, but during the song he turned his back on the wedding party. In his averted figure I saw the woman who forgot the dance, the land that rejected its own singers. I think I understood then the sad farce of Irish censorship, the modern middle-class commitment to complacency and swinish apathy, Joyce's nightmare, the ferocious bitterness of many Irish poets and artists I have met, the contemporary fear of the silence of the self (a grotesque parody of song is preferable to no song at all), and behind it all, the responsibility of the poet to explore and celebrate the entire thing. If "My Dark Fathers" achieves the clarity I hoped it would, that is what it means. Or at least, that is part of its significance, because no human

†This quotation and the three previous ones may be found in Frank O'Connor's *The Backward Look* (Macmillan, 1967), Chapter Eleven.

being can say exactly what a poem means. Only the poem can say that.

I believe there are many ways in which this responsibility can be fulfilled. The creation of comedy is one of them. Comedy turns suffering into laughter, desolation into sunniness. For my purposes, I find that the use of a character, a persona, Moloney, suits me well. In one poem he makes love to a girl on his mother's grave, which may also be "the pit of doom," the grave of song described in "My Dark Fathers." Moloney is a compendium of laughing men I have known. Laughter is sometimes courage, sometimes cowardice. Moloney is for me an attractive bundle of contradictions. I do not intend to let him fade.

I have said that I find poetry impossible to define, but that I would try to describe what it means to me. If this selection proves anything at all it is that poetry returns again and again to the same themes, like a ghost compelled to return and haunt endlessly a house that symbolizes everything it has known and loved. Poetry is an act of attention with the purpose of crystallizing a number of obsessions. I do not think that the poems in *Good Souls, to Survive* and *Dream of a Black Fox* are distinguished by a multiplicity of ideas or a wide range of emotions. No, they are deliberate repetitions of a few things that I have always found interesting: the attempt to understand the nature of good and evil; the essence of contradiction; the relationship of forces such as cruelty and corruption to the human passion and need for survival; the desirability of continuing, of sticking at it, of waking up again and walking out into the morning light; the ambiguous rewards of laughter;

the necessity for faith in youth even though it can be malevolent and stupid; the fact that man is blind and deformed. I like to write about things that move and sing and kill and generate—hounds, birds, badgers, tinkers, children, gossips. I am fascinated by the animated aimlessness of ordinary conversation; it seems to me a dishevelled rehearsal for a perfect play that never comes off. I believe that poetry is not only an act of attention, it is also an act of faith in the poet's capacity to begin again though there are many forces that would disrupt this process, bring it all to an end. Poetry will never finally solve anything because it is the voice of new promise, the art of permanent beginning. That is why I continue to write.

BRENDAN KENNELLY.

for Keene.

The Gift

It came slowly.
Afraid of insufficient self-content,
Or some inherent weakness in itself,
Small and hesitant,
Like children at the tops of stairs,
It came through shops, rooms, temples,
Streets, places that were badly-lit,
It was a gift that took me unawares
And I accepted it.

The House

The coldness that is water in the hour before the
  dawn;
Small girls in a side-street, faces held in hands
Softer than silence; noon-day dark; white night-
  light;
The broad hush round the pool where lean bulrushes
  sprout
And herons stand in water, covering young sands;
All, all became the force that lifewards drove his
  plight.
—Oh let him build his house of faith and doubt.

When was it first? Walking the green ways, round
  the edge of days
Grown into hills of water? Reaching deep, deep
Into the green of moss, drawing the blind down
On life's vague face, pale vision shall conclusions
  flout?
Or in small things that the impotent heart felt creep
Into a plan, forever held? In lights that drown?
—Oh let him build his house of faith and doubt.

He saw it once or twice: when the frail bull-calf,
  stumbling, fell
On the spiky light of evening, gored in wet
Grass, trembling in the white spirals of its breath;
When the broken bird rose, speared from the
  bracken, out
Into the air that, man-like, hastened to forget.

Twice. Tremor of limb, quiver of wing. Cold of
  death.
—Oh let him build his house of faith and doubt.

The vision arches upwards, pale vision known in
  young leaves;
Overarching all—dream, search and seeker. He
Stands now, looking at it, finding shadows, lights,
That are but part. Summers fade. Waters die in
  drought,
But, in the sunset, streams go spinning to the sea.
Meaning is in winter, life's walls that block our
  sights.
—The man has built his house of faith and doubt.

Sonnet

The negro smiled. His teeth showed white as snow.
His eyes stirred like the depths of muddy wine.
He said, "Back in Jamaica, I use' go
Pick coconut every mawnin'. Sun shine
Early, five, six o'clock maybe, an' we
Spend all day hackin'. Jus' hackin', man. Fine
Time we have, though. Sometimes, under a tree,
I sleep during day: always watch for sign
Of sun. Man, it was warm. At night, I lie
On sand with gal. Toss her hair. Laugh. And we
Sing a li'l. Now, she have ten chil'ren. I
Know she ugly now, like my mother." He
Paused and smiled again. "My mother fine. But
Man, she think whole world made of coconut."

A Drowned Girl

Waves' delicate fingers twined a tight noose of death
    around
Her beautiful body, destined, until then, to thrive;
When they scrambled her on to the rocks, she looked
    so young
You'd swear she was still alive.

She didn't look dead, but looked like any other girl
At whom you'd throw an admiring glance;
Quick brightness in a street, disturbing surprise at
    evening,
Frail truth in the impulse of the dance.

Heroisms happened swiftly; an old man, with bleed-
    ing toes,
Attempted things impossible alike to old and young;
Blew his stale breath between her frigid lips,
Too feeble to help stopped heart and water-stifled
    lung.

Doctor, priest, civilian prayed and probed and tried
To find one reassuring remnant of breath,
As if they couldn't see why a girl in a green swimsuit
Should be so irretrievably stretched in death.

There was no flood-tide of grief then, no cold con-
    sciousness
Of the essential tragedy, yet:

But the curious gaped, mumbled and stumbled
In a way impossible to forget.

Awareness wrapped itself like wet ropes of weed
	around the minds of all,
Rocks and beach became a mesmerized room,
And she, turning cold, looked somehow unwanted,
A blue child thrust from an impatient womb.

Various doctors pronounced her dead and everyone
	stood aside
While stretcher-bearers carried her from the rocks
	to a house on dry land;
Shortly afterwards, waves' delicate fingers twined
	white ribbons of foam
Around her footprints, perfect in the gentle sand . . .

The Birds

Beneath the stare of God's gold burning eye,
Two crisp hands clap; a thousand plover rise
And wheel across the meadows of the sky.

Black wings flash and gleam; a perfect white
Makes beautiful each rising breast,
Sovereign in the far-off miracle of flight.

Their terror is a lovely thing,
A sudden inspiration, exploding
In the thunder of each beating wing;

A startling rout, as of an army driven
In broken regiments
Against the proud, fantastic face of heaven.

And yet, no mad disorder, no raucous accident
Deforms the miracle; high flocks
Fulfil an inbred, furious intent.

In screams of dread, perfection whirls
Along the headlands of the sky.
They circle, gabbing now like girls,

And wing to safety in Carrig Wood,
Dip through branches, disappear. Across the sky,
The pale sun throws a quilt of solitude.

After terror, they are safety's prisoners,
Momentary victims of security
In labyrinths where surly winter stirs.

They breathe on branches, hidden and alone.
Fear will flare again, but now the abandoned sky
Is turning cold and grey as stone.

I think about that marvellous rout, that empty sky,
That flight of plover hidden from
The stare of God's gold burning eye.

The Dummies

Their restless hands articulate desire
In frantic gestures of meaning,
Fantastic patterns of the inner fire.

So it must have been among the first
Brothers—a frenzy of excitement
Before love, hate, hunger, thirst

Were named. Four dummies! Brothers too!
Each one in his particular silence
Creates bridges, trees, deep spaces through

Which he reaches to a brother, hungrily.
Outer beasts move in colourful confusion.
Brothers need each other, utterly.

The spirit's energy is their eloquence. Their
Animated hands mould marvellous
Expressions out of the simple air.

Yet, each one's unalterable separateness remains.
In tragic silence, each dumb soul
Is islanded in darkness of the city lanes.

Moloney Remembers the Resurrection of Kate Finucane

"O she was the handsome corpse," he said,
"Divil a difference between livin' and dead
You'd see in her; a fine red face
On a starchy pillow edged with lace,
Her cold hands clasped, her mousy hair
As neatly tied as a girl's at a fair.
Touchin' forty she was when she passed away,
But twenty she looked as she lay
In bed on the broad of her back.
Kate Finucane of Asdee West
Was stretched in death, but she looked her best!

                            Her cousins had come
From all parts of the Kingdom
For the wake; Coffeys and Lanes from Dingle,
McCarthys and Ryans, married and single,
Honest and otherwise. For a day and a night
As she lay in her bed, a sight
For sore eyes, they drank and they prayed
And they sang her to heaven—as fine
A wake as ever I went to in all my time!

Well, there was nothin' to do, after prayin' and
    drinkin',
But lift herself into the coffin.
'Twas at that moment, glory to God,
As I stood with my glass at the head
Of her bed, that she stretched like a cat and opened
    her eyes

And lifted her head in great surprise;
And motherogod will I ever forget
The cut an' the go, the sight an' the set
Of her when, calm as you like, with a toss of her
    head,
Kate Finucane sat up in the bed!

           No need to tell
Of all the confusion that fell
On the cousins, neighbours, myself and the house.
Dead she'd been, and now this disastrous
Return to life, upsettin' the whole
Place, and I thinkin' her body was lackin' a soul.
But after a while, things quietened down
And Kate made tea for the cousins. She found
She'd not seen them for ages. What's more,
She clapped her eye on a Lenamore
Man called Harty, and three months later,
Paraded him in rare style up to the altar!
On top o' that, she showed the world she could
Make a dandy wife, for she's still to the good,
And without doubt or favour, fright or fear,
Kate Finucane has a child a year!

"Gay woman, Kate," Moloney said,
"Divil a difference between livin' and dead!"

Moloney Up and At It

"My soul from hell, the night the ould wan died,"
Moloney said, "I cried and cried
Tears down. I'd been tied to her string
Through rack and hardship and the wild fling
Of youth, through manhood and the grey
Days when youth begins to slip away,
And now my addled heart and head
Were bound by the memory o' the dead.

Well, anyway, after puttin' herself down
In the box, I went to the town
O' Lishtowel for a few drinks, and there
I met a Knockanore woman with red hair
And gamey eye. I made bold
And in a short time had told
Her my story. She cocked her ear and listened well.
We drank until the darkness fell
And for hours after. The talk
Spun on love. 'Can I walk
A piece with you?' says I. 'Moloney,' says she,
'You're welcome to do what you like with me.'
Fair enough! We left Lishtowel and struck the road,
Footin' it free over pot-hole
And gravel. The Knockanore woman was full o' guff
And harped on all the tricks o' love.
I upped with the question. She
Was willin' and free.
'Where would you like it?' says I. 'Well,' she said,
'God's green earth is a warm bed.'
'Right you are, girl,' says I.

It happened we were passin' by
Gale graveyard where my mother lay.
'What would you say
To this place?' says I. 'Moloney,' says she,
'If it's right with you, it's right with me.'

Straightaway, I opened the gate and led
The Knockanore woman over the dead
O' seven parishes. Talk of a flyer!
Fast as they come and hot as fire!
She fell down on the soft clay
Of a fresh grave, and before I could say
A word, I was on the ground as well,
Goin' like the hammers o' hell!
'Twas only then I saw where I was.
On my mother's grave. But that was no cause
For panic, though I was a bit
Upset at first by the strangeness of it.
The Knockanore woman was happy as Larry,
And I was sparkin' and merry
As a cricket. 'Yerra, you might
As well enjoy the gift o' the night
While you have the chance,' I said
To myself, realizin' the dead are dead,
Past holiness and harms—
And the livin' woman was in my arms.

'Twas great fun
While it lasted, and it lasted long. The sun
Was startin' to climb the sky when we rose
Up and settled our clothes.

'How are you, girl?' says I.
'Yerra, fine,' says she.
' 'Twas a fine night,' says I
' 'Twas so, but a bit cold towards mornin',' says she,
'And I wouldn't mind a hot cup o' tay
This minute.' 'Whist,' I said,
Suddenly remembering the quiet dead.
With the memory, I started to sing,
Then and there, a bar of a jig,
And as I sang I danced as well
On the body whose soul was in heaven or hell.
'You're a gay man,' says she, 'to bring
Me to a place like this for your bit of a fling,
And I'm thinkin' the love has gone to your head
When you dance a jig on the bones o' the dead.'
Said I, 'By the Christ that is divine,
If I have a son may he dance on mine.
While a man has a chance he should dance and sing,'
    I said,
'For he'll be the hell of a long time dead.
So come on now without further ado
And I'll put on the kettle for the tay.'
She smiled and we started on our way
In the early light that was breaking for day.

The night was lost, the daylight stretched ahead,
Behind me lay the unforgettable dead,
Beside me walked a woman with gamey eye,
Laughing as the sun rose in the sky."

My Dark Fathers

My dark fathers lived the intolerable day
Committed always to the night of wrong,
Stiffened at the hearthstone, the woman lay,
Perished feet nailed to her man's breastbone.
Grim houses beckoned in the swelling gloom
Of Munster fields where the Atlantic night
Fettered the child within the pit of doom,
And everywhere a going down of light.

And yet upon the sandy Kerry shore
The woman once had danced at ebbing tide
Because she loved flute music—and still more
Because a lady wondered at the pride
Of one so humble. That was long before
The green plant withered by an evil chance;
When winds of hunger howled at every door
She heard the music dwindle and forgot the dance.

Such mercy as the wolf receives was hers
Whose dance became a rhythm in a grave,
Achieved beneath the thorny savage furze
That yellowed fiercely in a mountain cave.
Immune to pity, she, whose crime was love,
Crouched, shivered, searched the threatening sky,
Discovered ready signs, compelled to move
Her to her innocent appalling cry.

Skeletoned in darkness, my dark fathers lay
Unknown, and could not understand
The giant grief that trampled night and day,
The awful absence moping through the land.

Upon the headland, the encroaching sea
Left sand that hardened after tides of Spring,
No dancing feet disturbed its symmetry
And those who loved good music ceased to sing.

Since every moment of the clock
Accumulates to form a final name,
Since I am come of Kerry clay and rock,
I celebrate the darkness and the shame
That could compel a man to turn his face
Against the wall, withdrawn from light so strong
And undeceiving, spancelled in a place
Of unapplauding hands and broken song.

The Blind Man

Dark from birth,
And therefore spared the shock
Of losing light, not having known its worth.
I am aware of darkness round the clock,
A velvet kingdom, limits undefined,
Where touch, smell, ear equip me well.
Fastidiously, I try the noisy grind,
The aimless gusto of external hell.

I walk the inner alleys night and day,
Explore the salty laneways of the blood,
Note weeds and grasses, refuse thrown away,
Deduce what's evil, beautiful or good.
I move down sidestreets of the marrowbone,
Go moodily along its thoroughfare
On which the sun has sometimes shone;
And therefore I am blithe and debonair.

I've been informed of the things I miss:
Birds that steadily attempt the air,
Peculiar tints of whiskey in a glass,
Surprising sunlight in a woman's hair;
Shells half-buried in the sand
Originally spawned at sea,
Nature's gayest finery and
Casual phenomena of every day.

But vision is not simply seeing straight,
And things discoverable without exist within.
My shells and birds are different, yet elate
Me utterly. Images that spin

Within these limits are my own,
With colours, shapes and forms that I create,
Discovered somewhere in the blood and bone—
I only see whatever I can make.

Therefore I accept dark privacy;
I move beyond each voice
Which, unaware, asserts I cannot see.
While they acclaim, reproach, commend, rejoice,
I go among them, prodding the strange air,
Awkwardly involved while still outside,
Conscious of the things I'm fit to share,
Acknowledging the light I've been denied.

Getting Up Early

Getting up early promises well:
  A milkhorse on the road
Induces thoughts of a sleeping world
  And a waking God.

This hour has something sacred;
  Bells will be ringing soon,
But now I am content to watch
  The day begin to bloom.

I would only waste my breath
  On poor superfluous words;
How perfectly they sing for me—
  The new invisible birds

Who celebrate the light that spreads
  Like love to window sills,
As morning steps like a laughing girl
  Down from the Dublin hills.

C

Lislaughtin Abbey

Flashing starlings twist and turn
   In the sky above my head
While in Lislaughtin Abbey lie
   The packed anticipating dead.

Silent generations there
   That long had bent the knee
Endow the Shannon with the grace
   Of reaching to the sea.

Swollen by the rich juice of the dead,
   The Shannon moves with ease
Towards a mighty union with
   Atlantic mysteries.

But though the river sweeps beyond
   Each congested bone,
Its currents do not swirl towards
   A resurrection,

Any more than starlings do
   That, fearing death this winter day,
Create small thunder in the sky
   And shelter where they may,

Ignoring green Lislaughtin where
   Subtle shadows pass
Through shattered altars, broken walls,
   The blood of martyrs in the grass,

Into the ground that winters well
    And blossoms soon or late,
Preserving patient multitudes
    Who are content to wait

Till they at last disturb the stones,
    The fox's lair, the starling's nest,
To cry out with the howling damned,
    To wonder with the Blessed,

To hear the word for which they wait
    Under the coarse grass
The meanest blade of which assists
    In what must come to pass,

To see why silent centuries
    Have finally sufficed
To purge all in the rising flood
    Of the overflowing blood of Christ.

Restless at the gate, I turn away
    Groping towards what can't be said
And know I know but little
    Of the birds, the river and the dead.

The Good

(For Eavan)

The good are vulnerable
As any bird in flight.
They do not think of safety,
Are blind to possible extinction
And when most vulnerable
Are most themselves.
The good are real as the sun,
Are best perceived through clouds
Of casual corruption
That cannot kill the luminous sufficiency
That shines on city, sea and wilderness,
Fastidiously revealing
One man to another,
Who yet will not accept
Responsibilities of light.
The good incline to praise,
To have the knack of seeing that
The best is not destroyed
Although forever threatened.
The good go naked in all weathers,
And by their nakedness rebuke
The small protective sanities
That hide men from themselves.
The good are difficult to see
Though open, rare, destructible.
Always, they retain a kind of youth,
The vulnerable grace
Of any bird in flight,
Content to be itself,

Accomplished master and potential victim,
Accepting what the earth or sky intends.
I think that I know one or two
Among my friends.

Light Dying

In Memoriam Frank O'Connor (Michael O'Donovan)

Climbing the last steps to your house, I knew
That I would find you in your chair,
Watching the light die along the canal,
Recalling the glad creators, all
Who'd played a part in the miracle.
A silver-haired remembering king, superb there
In dying light, all ghosts being at your beck and call,
You made them speak as only you could do

Of generosity or loneliness or love
Because, you said, all men are voices, heard
In the pure air of the imagination.
I hear you now, your rich voice deep and kind,
Rescuing a poem from time, bringing to mind
Lost centuries with a summoning word,
Lavishing on us who need much more of
What you gave, glimpses of heroic vision.

So you were angry at the pulling down
Of what recalled a finer age; you tried
To show how certain things destroyed, ignored,
Neglected was a crime against the past,
Impoverished the present. Some midland town
Attracted you, you stood in the waste
Places of an old church and, profoundly stirred,
Pondered how you could save what time had sorely
        tried.

Or else you cried in rage against the force
That would reduce to barren silence all
Who would articulate dark Ireland's soul;
You knew the evil of the pious curse,
The hearts that make God pitifully small
Until He seems the God of little fear
And not the God that you desired at all;
And yet you had the heart to do and dare.

I see you standing at your window,
Lifting a glass, watching the dying light
Along the quiet canal bank come and go
Until the time has come to say good-night.
You see me to the door; you lift a hand
Half-shyly, awkwardly, while I remark
Your soul's fine courtesy, my friend, and
Walk outside, alone, suddenly in the dark.

But in the dark or no, I realise
Your life's transcendent dignity,
A thing more wonderful than April skies
Emerging in compelling majesty,
Leaving mad March behind and making bloom
Each flower outstripping every weed and thorn.
Life rises from the crowded clay of doom.
Light dying promises the light re-born.

Moments When the Light

There are moments when the light
Makes me start up, fright
In my heart as if I feared to see
Unbearable clarity about me.
Once, on Portobello Bridge,
I had the sudden privilege
Of seeing light leap from the sky
About five o'clock on an autumn day,
Defining every visible thing,
Unseen by one among the moving throng:
Road, bridge, factory, canal,
Stained swans and filthy reeds, all
The set homegoing faces
Filling motorcars and buses.
Then I knew that energy is but
Unconsciousness. If moving men could
See where they are going, they would
Stop and contemplate the light
And never move again until
They understood why it is should spill
A sudden benediction on
The head of every homegoing man.
But no-one looked or saw the way
The waters danced for the visiting light
Or how green foliage glittered. It
Was ignored completely.
I knew the world is most at ease
With acceptable insanities,
Important nothings that command
The heart and mind of busy men
Who, had they seen it, might have praised

The light on Portobello Bridge.
But then, light broke. I looked. An evening glow.
Men go home because they do not know.

Hunchback

Day after twisted day, I carry it on
My back—this devil's hump, this mound
Of misery sprung from the roots in
My body's clay, grotesque companion
Of my wildest dreams. I have to bend
Beneath it, flame and rage
Because distortion is my closest friend,
The faithful ally of my youth and age.

Along the quays I walk and watch
The seagulls climbing in their flight
Or skimming the slow Liffey. Such
Perfection hurts my blood. In broad daylight,
My ugliness gapes like a wound while I,
Hands rammed in empty pockets, see
White miracles of grace on every side.
They circle to astonish and torment me.

Torment eats my heart. I see small ships
From Hamburg, Copenhagen. A sailor
Gamecocks on an upper deck. My lips
Form silently the names—Regina,
Honor Belle. Ships are women, queens
That ride the ocean, plough the sea,
Leaving the white foam of unrest where they have
    been,
Hacking hard voyages from port to port in me.

The outside world explores me but I
Am unknown territory, a secret river
Of obscure source, uncertain estuary.
I flow through time that time may yet deliver
Me from myself, my sense of well-made
Manhood from monstrous flesh and bone.
Creation preens itself, neat planets are displayed,
Jupiter wheels above me. I move alone.

The Liberties, Townsend Street, Stephen's Green,
Stations in my shuffling odyssey
Of old, appalling loneliness and pain;
While girls grow up and boys put out to sea
And women shape new histories in the womb,
I walk the streets of failure day and night,
Watching the symmetries life must assume,
Easy ships at anchor, able birds in flight.

O shapely world that I'm compelled to see
But be no part of, I move
Through your designs deliberately.
I feel a certain love
For what I see but cannot linger on:
Wet pavements shine at night, clean church-bells
    ring,
I stand where multitudes have come and gone—
The parody best proves the real thing.

The Limerick Train

Hurtling between hedges now, I see
Green desolation stretch on either hand
While sunlight blesses all magnanimously.

The gods and heroes are gone for good and
Men evacuate each Munster valley
And midland plain, gravelly Connaught land

And Leinster town. Who, I wonder, fully
Understands the imminent predicament,
Sprung from rooted suffering and folly?

Broken castles tower, lost order's monument,
Splendour crumbling in sun and rain,
Witnesses to all we've squandered and spent,

But no Phoenix rises from that ruin
Although the wild furze in yellow pride
Explodes in bloom above each weed and stone,

Promise ablaze on every mountainside
After the centuries' game of pitch-and-toss
Separates what must live from what has died.

A church whips past, proclaiming heavy loss
Amounting to some forty thousand pounds;
A marble Christ unpaid for on His Cross

Accepts the Limerick train's irreverent sound,
Relinquishes great power to little men—
A river flowing still, but underground.

Wheels clip the quiet counties. Now and then
I see a field where like an effigy
In rushy earth, there stands a man alone

Lifting his hand in salutation. He
Disappears almost as soon as he is seen,
Drowned in distant anonymity.

We have travelled far, the journey has been
Costly, tormented odyssey through night;
And now, noting the unmistakable green,

The pools and trees that spring into the sight,
The sheep that scatter madly, wheel and run,
Quickly transformed to terrified leaping white,

I think of what the land has undergone
And find the luminous events of history
Intolerable as staring at the sun.

Only twenty miles to go and I'll be
Home. Seeing two crows low over the land,
I recognize the land's uncertainty,

The unsensational surrender and
Genuflection to the busy stranger
Whose power in pocket brings him power in hand.

Realizing now how dead is anger
Such as sustained us at the very start
With possibility in time of danger,

I know why we have turned away, apart
(I'm moving still but so much time has sped)
From the dark realities of the heart.

From my window now, I try to look ahead
And know, remembering what's been done and
    said,
That we must always cherish, and reject, the dead.

The Stallion

Outside the church the ribboned stallion stands,
The proud-as-Lucifer farmer at his head,
Hard reins of dominion in his hands.
The crowd have prayed for their remembered dead
And now they gaze upon the champing brute,
Changing from prayer to admiration
Of the great curved back, the shining cut
Of limb and flank, the massive pattern
Of bone and muscle in the morning sun.
The stallion lifts his head, a glossy king,
And rolls his eyes at many a farmer there
Who sizes up the animal coldly, then
Forgetting life and death and everything,
Thinks of that stallion spraddled on a likely mare.

The Image of God

Mulcaire was left a cripple in the heel of the hunt,
Badger-grey, suffering his eightieth year,
Tied to a sugawn chair, bearing the brunt
Of pain. When I knew him, his end was near.

The worm of memory gnawed at his rickety brain.
By day, he sat in the sun, stiffly apart.
At night, he stretched in his bed of pain,
Tired eyes failing to pierce the brutal dark,

Fingering, through the dead hours, his greasy beads,
Mouthing his pitiful prayers to some image of God,
Decaying alone in the dark. The tatters and shreds
Of his life came as always, it seemed, to no good.

His tongue was foul at times; he'd curse
The passers-by who threw him the pitying look,
He'd light the ground with oaths at others, or worse,
Spit scorn on neighbour and stranger till his body shook.

"I'm dead from the bloody shakes" he'd say
Lifting his trembling hands to your face,
"But I was a tradesman once and there was a day
I was hailed for my skill in this benighted place."

His hands shook madly as he struggled to light
The crooked briar pipe he sucked as though
It yielded some saving ration of life
To the body that thinned and wasted day after day.

The bit of scandal to him was as good as bread,
The misfortune of others, perhaps, softened his own:
"The Murphy wan had a bastard, born dead,
Ah, Christ, but the women love a prod of the bone!"

Under it all, the tide of his suffering ran,
Ravaging, black, chilling his cranky blood;
He died in winter alone, a smelly old man
Who was made, according to some, in the image of God.

Blackbird

This shiny forager cocks his head
As if listening for the sound
Of killable phenomena
Underground.

He depends entirely
On the sharp eye and ear,
On the ravening stab
Of a yellow beak

From which just now,
Spontaneous as light, pure as flame,
Impassioning the chill day,
Such music came

I scarce believe his murderous competence
As he stabs to stay alive,
Choking music
That music may survive.

Good Souls, to Survive

Things inside things endure
Longer than things exposed;
We see because we are blind
And should not be surprised to find
We survive because we're enclosed.

If merit is measured at all,
Vulnerability is the measure.
The little desire protection
With something approaching passion,
Will not be injured, cannot face error.

So the bird in astonishing flight
Chokes on the stricken blood,
The bull in the dust is one
With surrendered flesh and bone,
Naked on chill wood.

The real is rightly intolerable,
Its countenance stark and abrupt.
Good souls, to survive, select
Their symbols from among the elect—
Articulate, suave, corrupt.

But from corruption comes the deep
Desire to plunge to the true;
To dare is to redeem the blood,
Discover the buried good,
Be vulnerably new.

Three Men

PEARSE

Walking the indifferent streets
 Or the green deserts of the west,
He chose impossibility
Imaged in a burning town;
Later, things were possible,
When in the Easter test
Flames of change leaped up
From houses crashing down.

2

PLUNKETT

Surely Joseph Plunkett was right
To take Grace Gifford for a bride
In the untold desolation
Of the morning that he died.
She, lover, wife and widow
Almost in a single breath,
Understood. He, tautly poised
Upon the threshold of his death,
Knew simply that in little time
He'd stretch to frenzied lead,
Prone, alone on the barrack square,
His unshared bridal bed.

3

MACDONAGH

Seeing the blackbird, yellowhammer, crane,
He was not moved,
But the yellow bittern,
Shy and apart, he loved.
How deftly it picked its way
Over marshland, rock and stone,
Audaciously climbing the sky,
Braving the sea alone.

Planner of the burning town,
Bridegroom of an hour
And lover of the shy, wild bird
Discovered death, remain unknown;
As do, perhaps, all those
Who, losing touch with others,
Retrieve what is their own.

The Teachers

How brilliantly they teach me
What I would love to learn—
An idiom of ecstasy.

The spread of an accomplished wing
Gives a tongue to their silence,
Wrings words from me, wondering

At their expertise
As they skim roof-tops, swoop streetwards,
Ride high on the back of a breeze

In their didactic flight
Over ignorant cities, instructing us to praise
The nonchalant and exquisite.

But they cry out sometimes, fearfully
It seems, as if in soaring
Up from earth, they could see

Spread out beneath them, like rows and rows of dead,
Hungry people of many lands
Crying out for bread.

Then I hear the language of hunger
And see the bleak famine-words
Stamped on the starving air

And hands reaching for the birds
That scream and sway into the sky,
Spreading the tragic word.

O every swift master, high teacher,
I grasp your secret idiom—
Ecstasy, hunger.

Begin

Begin again to the carolling birds,
To the sight of light at the window,
Begin to the roar of morning traffic
All along Pembroke Road.
Every beginning is a promise
Born in light and dying in dark,
Daily deception and exultation
Of Springtime flowering the way to work.
Begin to the pageant of queueing girls,
To the lonely arrogance of swans in the canal,
To bridges linking the past and future,
To old friends passing though with us still.
Begin to the treasures that we have squandered,
To the profit and loss, the pleasure and pain,
Begin to the knowledge that to-morrow
Is another beginning for every man.
Begin to the loneliness that cannot end
Since it perhaps is what makes us begin,
Begin to wonder at unknown faces,
At crying birds and the sudden rain,
At branches stark in the winter sunlight,
At seagulls foraging for bread,
At couples sharing a sunny secret
Alone together while making good.
Begin to the surge of the waking city,
To familiar streets that are always strange,
To words of greeting in the Dublin morning
Proving that we have come through again.
Blessed with the promise and disappointment
That make the minutes of every day,

We step into the streets of morning
Walking the pavements of come-what-may.
Though we live in a world that thinks of ending,
That always seems about to give in,
Something that will not acknowledge conclusion
Insists what we forever begin.

The Tippler

Out of the clean bones
He tipples a hard music.
Cocking his head,
He knows himself sole master of his trade.
Hence his pride.

A goat ran wild
Through field and hillside,
Was tracked, caught, tethered, tamed,
Butchered and no man cried.
And the Tippler got his bones.

All bones dry in the sun,
Harden to browny white,
Mere flesh stripped and gone;
But bones create a new delight
When clacked by the proper man.

Let flesh lie rotten
When the Tippler takes his stand,
Holds the bones between his fingers;
Death has given him command,
Permitted him his hunger,

Made his heart articulate,
Tender, proud,
Clacking at shoulder, chest and head.
That man is for a while unbowed
Who brings music from the dead.

The Pig-Killer

On the scoured table, the pig lies
On its back, its legs held down
By Ned Gorman and Joe Dineen.
Over its throat, knife in hand, towers

Fitzmaurice, coatless, his face and hands
Brown as wet hay. He has travelled
Seven miles for this kill and now,
Eager to do a good job, examines

The prone bulk. Tenderly his fingers move
On the flabby neck, seeking the right spot
For the knife. Finding it, he leans
Nearer and nearer the waiting throat,

Expert fingers fondling flesh. Nodding then
To Gorman and Dineen, he raises the knife,
Begins to trace a line along the throat.
Slowly the line turns red, the first sign

Of blood appears, spreads shyly over the skin. The
    pig
Begins to scream. Fitzmaurice halts his blade
In the middle of the red line, lifts it slightly,
Plunges it eight inches deep

Into the pig. In a flash, the brown hands
Are red, and the pig's screams
Rise and fall with the leaping blood. The great heaving
Body relaxes for Gorman and Dineen.

Fitzmaurice stands back, lays his knife on
A window-sill, asks for hot water and soap.
Blade and hands he vigorously purges, then
Slipping on his battered coat,

Eyeing the pig, says with authority—
"Dead as a doornail! Still as a mouse!
There's a good winter's feedin' in that baishte!"
Fitzmaurice turns and strides into the house.

Union

When salmon swarmed in the brown tides
And cocks raised their lusty din
And her heart beat like a wild bird's heart,
She left her kin.

A black ass brayed in the village,
Men ploughed and mowed,
There was talk of rising water
When he struck the road.

Words stranger than were scattered
Over the shuttered dead
Were faint as child-songs in their ears
When they stretched in bed.

A Kerry Christmas

The frost transfigures and the wind deceives,
A warring season bickers to its end,
The exiles gather and the land believes
It knows a birth, commemorates a friend
Who scatters crumbs of love to north and south,
Countering the scrounging winter light;
Goodwill dribbles from the swilling mouth,
The mad Atlantic thrashes in the night

Where Mollie Conner, shawled in total black,
The smell of clay telling where she has been,
A cross of generation on her back,
Nourished by the long, resurgent story
Explaining what ecstatic voices mean,
Stumbles to her private, certain glory.

The Stones

Worried mothers bawled her name
To call wild children from their games.

"Nellie Mulcahy! Nellie Mulcahy!
If ye don't come home,
She'll carry ye off in her big black bag."

Her name was fear and fear begat obedience,
But one day she made a real appearance—
A harmless hag with a bag on her back.
When the children heard, they gathered together
And in a trice were
Stalking the little weary traveller—
Ten, twenty, thirty, forty.
Numbers gave them courage
Though, had they known it,
Nellie was more timid by far
Than the timidest there.
Once or twice, she turned to look
At the bravado-swollen pack.
Slowly the chant began—

"Nellie Mulcahy! Nellie Mulcahy!
Wicked old woman! Wicked old woman!"

One child threw a stone.
Another did likewise.
Soon the little monsters
Were furiously stoning her
Whose name was fear.
When she fell bleeding to the ground,

Whimpering like a beaten pup,
Even then they didn't give up
But pelted her like mad.

Suddenly they stopped, looked at
Each other, then at Nellie, lying
On the ground, shivering.

Slowly they withdrew
One by one.

Silence. Silence.
All the stones were thrown.

Between the hedges of their guilt
Cain-children shambled home.

Alone,
She dragged herself up,
Crying in small half-uttered moans,
Limped away across the land,
Black bag on her back,
Agony racking her bones.

Between her and the children,
Like hideous forms of fear—
The stones.

The Thatcher

He whittled scallops for a hardy thatch,
His palm and fingers hard as the bog oak.
You'd see him of an evening, crouched
Under a tree, testing a branch. If it broke
He grunted in contempt and flung it away,
But if it stood the stretch, his sunken blue
Eyes briefly smiled. Then with his long knife he
Chipped, slashed, pointed. The pile of scallops grew.

Astride a house on a promised day,
He rammed and patted scallops into place
Though wind cut his eyes till he seemed to weep.
Like a god after making a world, his face
Grave with the secret, he'd stare and say—
"Let the wind rip and the rain pelt. This'll keep."

The Song Inside

The caged bird sang his heart out all day long.
His cage was freedom and his freedom sang.

Inside a shut window hung the cage.
The room resounded with the privilege.

Sometimes I closed my eyes to see
It better, to hear its purity—

Note after heart-enrapturing note
Pour from the masterful sleek throat.

In silent heaven, a killer spread
His wings—murder in his golden head.

Sovereign in his blue territory,
Did, nevertheless, fix his eye

On the caged bird. On high,
Poised in murderous mastery,

He watched, watched, knifed the air.
Death whistled, flourished everywhere.

The room darkened like a tomb,
The golden body dispensing doom

Found all doom in itself,
Hurtling blindly at the glass

That separated this strange pair—
Caged singer, golden killer.

Flare of terror. Soon, again, the song inside.
Outside, the hawk was dead.

The Grip

In Moynihan's meadow
The badger turned on the hound
And gripped.

The hound bit and tore
At the badger's body.
Harder, harder
The badger gripped.

The men ran up.
O'Carroll shouted "Quick! Quick! Crack a stick."

The stick cracked.
Deceived,
The iron jaws relaxed.

The hurt hound bit in fury.
Again the badger
Gripped.
The neck, this time.

No loosening now.
Fangs tightened in a fierce embrace
Of vein and sinew.
No complex expertise, no difficult method,
No subtle undermining, no lying guile,

Only the simple savage style

As the hound weakened, slumped, died.
The white teeth parted
Red with the fresh blood.

The men watched him turn,
Head for a hedge,
Low grey killer,
Skin ripped from sides, back, head, neck.

O'Carroll prodded the dead hound
With a blackthorn stick,
Said, more to himself than to others
Standing there—

"A hundred hurts are bad
But a good grip
Will break the heart
Of the best hound in the land."

A Drama

A summer's day: an old man sits in the shade,
Leathery effigy chewing the cud of dream—
A quiet drama privately staged in his head,
Greyed by things that are, saved by things that seem.

A dog lopes into the street where an oily bitch
Sweats as she waits, her steaming tongue hanging out.
He circles, smells her, circles again with such
Deliberate care, it seems his heart is in doubt.

He mounts of a sudden, expertly spraddles the brute,
His head at her back, scaring the busy flies.
The old man's drama suddenly switches to youth,
The dogs' rhythm increases, he closes his eyes.

In the shade of the castle, the meadowscent was
       sweet,
The bitch that he mounted then he cannot recall,
The pure daylight, the freedom, the summery sweat,
The rising desire he believed would not end at all.

But it did . . . and he opens his eyes to the day,
To the dogs that do it, unconscious of living or dead;
A woman passes and turns her eyes away,
He watches, knows there is nothing to say,
The vice of dream tightens his dying head.

A Special Odour

Up from the Sunday morning river drifts
A special odour of corruption,
The Dublin fog of foulness never lifts,
The dead are abed,
The living seek their temples of delusion.

Devil a god would smile to see
The rot beneath the elegance,
The serpent slander that last night stung humanity
Lies coiled in sleep.
And now the hour of holy impotence.

If one must offer any prayer
To much-beleaguered heaven—
Preserve your sense of humour, be merciful and fair,
For only God's wild laughter
Could hope that things will turn out even.

Very soon, I'll up and take a walk
Along a route I have not planned,
I'll think of Dublin's treacherous talk
And its malignant silences.
I will not understand.

Not that I give a tinker's curse.
I'll idle by the river's edge and see
The depths where nameless things rehearse
In dark dumb-show, sad human roles—
Slimed, active, predatory,

Conducting unrecorded slaughter
With viciously accomplished skill
In worlds arrested underwater,
Teaching one another
Convenient ways to kill.

At the Party

When the woman at the party said
That she was dying of some incurable disease,
I stared into my glass and saw the red
Wine's glittering infinities
Dancing alive between my fingers,
Making me again confront her eyes—
No traces there of any special hunger,
No painful guess, hysterical surmise.
She said, "Christmas in this land is cold,
Maguire's idea to go abroad is good;
As for myself, I like to take a stroll
On winter afternoons. Always heats the blood."
Barely hearing, I agreed. She smiled again.
Her world approached, touched, recoiled from mine.
The room was loud with noise of dying men.
Her parted lips accepted the good wine.

Ice

To-day I saw the ice
Whitening the world, killing the grass,
Ruthlessly piling loss

On loss. The papers said
A man stepped out to push his car
And was frozen dead.

But I saw the thrush and blackbird,
Proud as you like, step kingly to my door,
Cocking their heads for bread.

Crusts I threw to the cold singers
Who ventured near, like poets
Shy to tell their hunger

But quick to take the proffered fare.
Later, by a lake,
I saw a child at the edge where

The ice was just beginning to break;
He wanted to clutch and smash the ice
But someone snapped "For Christ's sake

Draw back, the ice is thin!"
It was, though farther out
Seagulls stood on the water's skin

Like unperturbed ambassadors who know
Just how deep appearances are
And how far they can go

Till the ice breaks under their feet.
And I thought
Of its purity and threat—

How it kills and cleans, petrifies
And purges, locks, tightens, chokes
And then melts in the sun's rays,

To draw the singers from my door
Back to sky and field;
To let the daring child once more

Resume his human privilege
Of breaking the rule that says he must
Not go too near the edge.

A Visit

No. 10 bus to the Park.
The conductor gives his promised shout
I enter the house of the mad.

A late March day. The sun
Warms my back as I go in.
They sit, stand, walk, stare. Are alone.

No sharing this loneliness.
Unrelatedness
Is the skin on every face.

Unrelatedness.
I'd like to smash through this,
But find only an abyss. An abyss.

I've come to see a man.
I find him in the garden.
Flowers flourish all about him

But he is withering now,
Failing away from me.
I am stupid, cut off. How

Can I suggest a link?
I can neither speak nor think.
He speaks though, his eyes sunk

In his head.
Something about dolls he has made.
All around, the unreachable mad.

He has painted pictures too.
They cover the walls of his room.
Maybe I should see them sometime?

Yes I would. What are they about?
He can't say that.
I'll find out.

So.
After silence, I must go.
What else can I do?

As if I'd never been he sits there.
Mad flowers bloom everywhere.
Men and women stare at me. They stare.

Girl in a Rope

By the still canal
She enters a slack rope,
Moves, slowly at first, round and round;
Gathering speed,
(Faster, faster now)
She clips the air without a sound—
Swift whirling sight,
Creator of a high design,
Orbiting in sheer delight
The red and white No Parking sign.

Dream of a Black Fox

The black fox loped out of the hills
And circled for several hours,
Eyes bright with menace, teeth
White in the light, tail dragging the ground.
The woman in my arms cringed with fear,
Collapsed crying, her head hurting my neck.
She became dumb fear.

The black fox, big as a pony,
Circled and circled,
Whimsical executioner,
Torment dripping like saliva from its jaws.
Too afraid to show my fear,
I watched it as it circled;
Then it leaped across me
Its great black body breaking the air,
Landing on a wall above my head.

Turning then, it looked at me.

And I saw it was magnificent,
Ruling the darkness, lord of its element,
Scorning all who are afraid,
Seeming even to smile
At human pettiness and fear.

The woman in my arms looked up
At this lord of darkness
And as quickly hid her head again.

Then the fox turned and was gone
Leaving us with fear
And safety—
Every usual illusion.

Quiet now, no longer trembling,
She lay in my arms,
Still as a sleeping child.

I knew I had seen fear,
Fear dispelled by what makes fear
A part of pure creation.
It might have taught me
Mastery of myself,
Dominion over death,
But was content to leap
With ease and majesty
Across the valleys and the hills of sleep.

A Man I Knew

(i.m. Patrick Kavanagh)

(1)

"I want no easy grave" he said to me,
"Where those who hated me can come and stare,
Slip down upon a servile knee,
Muttering their phoney public prayer.
In the wilds of Norfolk I'd like to lie,
No commemorative stone, no sheltering trees,
Far from the hypocrite's tongue and eye,
Safe from the praise of my enemies."

(2)

A man I knew who seemed to me
The epitome of chivalry
Was constantly misunderstood.
The heart's dialogue with God
Was his life's theme and he
Explored its depths assiduously
And without rest. Therefore he spat
On every shoddy value that
Blinded men to their true destiny—
The evil power of mediocrity,
The safety of the barren pose,
All that distorted natural grace.
Which is to say, almost everything.
Once he asked a girl to sing
A medieval ballad. As her voice rang out,
She was affronted by some interfering lout.

This man I knew spat in his face
And wished him to the floor of hell.
I thought then, and still think it well
That man should wear the spittle of disgrace
For violating certain laws.

Now I recall my friend because
He lived according to his code
And in his way was true to God.
Courage he had and was content to be
Himself, whatever came his way.
There is no other chivalry.

Birthdays and Farewells

Birthdays and farewells—what are they
But parodies of two
Realities that we
Pass through?

So away with "One year older!"
And "Farewell, sweetheart!"—
Let numbered candles melt,
All trains depart;

Perish the predictable joy,
Fling moist words to the nearest wind.
Other encounters and departures claim
A hearing in the mind.

Hear them, and forget
The coy table, the valedictory light,
The fake rehearsals that we make
For death's opening night.

Night-Drive

I

The rain hammered as we drove
Along the road to Limerick.
"Jesus what a night" Alan breathed
And—"I wonder how he is, the last account
Was poor."
I couldn't speak.

The windscreen fumed and blurred, the rain's spit
Lashing the glass. Once or twice
The wind's fist seemed to lift the car
And pitch it hard against the ditch.
Alan straightened out in time,
Silent. Glimpses of the Shannon—
A boiling madhouse roaring for its life
Or any life too near its gaping maw,
White shreds flaring in the waste
Of insane murderous black;
Trees bending in grotesque humility,
Branches scattered on the road, smashed
Beneath the wheels.
Then, ghastly under headlights,
Frogs bellied everywhere, driven
From the swampy fields and meadows,
Bewildered refugees, gorged with terror,
Dispossessed, obscene, plopping into death.
We killed them because we had to,
Their fatness crunched and flattened in the dark.
"How is he now?" Alan whispered

To himself. Behind us,
Foul carnage of broken frogs.

II

His head
Sweated on the pillow of the white hospital bed.
He spoke a little, said
Outrageously, "I think I'll make it."
Another time, he'd rail against the weather,
(Such a night would make him eloquent)
But now, quiet, he gathered his fierce will
To live.

III

Coming home
Alan saw the frogs.
"Look at them, they're everywhere,
Dozens of the bastards dead."

Minutes later—
"I think he might pull through now."
Alan, thoughtful at the wheel, was picking out
The homeroad in the flailing rain.
Night-hedges closed on either side.
In the suffocating darkness
I heard the heavy breathing
Of my father's pain.

Ghosts

The loved, articulate ghosts
Are no use now,
The noble encouragers are silent,
Self-sufficient on the mountain.

Choir and hosanna
Celebrate
The voices whose purity is proved,
The silence I must break.

This is as it should be.
Words
Define the heart as fiercely
As death defines a man
Or as the sea defines a shell.

At the Shannon's edge to-day
I saw a hundred birds in flight.
"Look!" my brother said, "clap your hands.
Their back is black.
And clap again,
Their belly's white.
Can you beat that, boy!"

No, I can't beat that. Brother,
When I consider
The perfect creatures of the air,
I know there's little I can beat
Or ever want to. Yet,
Mindful of those ghosts
Who have achieved a mighty silence,

Respecting the definition of death
And the sea's untiring style,
Desiring the precision of birds
That flash from black to white,

I look within, without,
And write.

Gestures

She passed me on the street
Her hand a quick white arc
Motioning brown hair—
Sweet Narcissus vanished in the crowd.

A girl that I knew better
Her mouth twisted in rage
Closed her eyes of a sudden
And stared at her own darkness.

One I love
Walked on a summer strand,
Bent and picked a shell,
Remarked on its intricacy,
Its scrupulous profundity,
Then tossed it into the sea.

Myself when young
Crouched near a rough mud wall
Seeking a sheltering shade
And covered my face with my hands.
Afraid.

Only gestures remain
To tell me the truth of things,
To grasp the flashing essences
That leap, scatter and die;
Only simple gestures
Confound the usual lie.

Secrets

Though most of the world I see
And continue to look at
Lives for the ugly

Secrets live to be told.
Hard to believe!
Everywhere young and old

Yawn in their mortal boredom,
Hearts melting forth with their breath,
Mouths frozen and dumb.

It is time we yielded to secrets
Waiting in faces, in grey strips of road,
Streets where crowds shove day and night

As if there were something to reach for.
Preparing for this
Delicate constant surrender

To flames and their brief whisperings,
To shores where the light
X-rays a gull's wings

And the outraged sea
Spews back the poison
It took from humanity

Locked in rooms that have known
More than would be revealed
If the flesh were stripped from the bone,

Demands a deliberate slowing,
A scrupulous prelude
To loving and knowing,

Something more than mere conscious art,
A sustained ritual
Of the open heart.

So from the peak
Of our redemption we permit
Secrets to speak

Through the ripe pear that will soon fall,
The candle melting on the stair,
The bird's quick shadow on the bedroom wall.

Bread

Someone else cut off my head
In a golden field.
Now I am re-created

By her fingers. This
Moulding is more delicate
Than a first kiss,

More deliberate than her own
Rising up
And lying down.

Even at my weakest, I am
Finer than anything
In this legendary garden

Yet I am nothing till
She runs her fingers through me
And shapes me with her skill.

The form that I shall bear
Grows round and white.
It seems I comfort her

Even as she slits my face
And stabs my chest.
Her feeling for perfection is

Absolute.
So I am glad to go through fire
And come out

Shaped like her dream.
In my way
I am all that can happen to men.
I came to life at her fingerends.
I will go back into her again.

So

When you hear a cry begin
To hurt the heart, you bid it
Return to its origin

Of peace. When you see
A shadow twisting on the wall
You let it through you

Like sunlight through a mountain stream
Showing black gravel
On the bed. When someone seems

Unhappy you recognize
It as the poisonweed
That floats on the white

Breaking crest of the wave
Knowing it rises only
To slip into its grave.

If a neighbour drinks herself to death
Sitting in her room,
You celebrate the holy breath

Of life in her, the sweet
Undying joy in all her dying blood.
I've seen the city sweat

In its futility, you find a calm
In its malignant storm.
The gulls' white cries of terror ram

The wind, the dog dies
At man's progressive hand,
This year the crop of lies

Choked many fields. You turned aside
From the corrupt streets, hurt
That certain things had died,

Yet with a tribute in the blood
Because what is is so,
Because what is is good.

Question

It is some time now since
We made up our minds
To leave the islands,

Black cliffs glinting with
More majesty than cathedral
Pillars in sunlight,

Green summits warm in summer
When the sheep grazed
But pure in winter

When the snow
Reached behind our eyes
Inspiring vertigo.

There was no need to tell
Ourselves what the islands were;
Always virginal

Resisting the sea's rape,
Green tabernacles
Under lightning and thunderclap

And the waves' repeated prayer
Or insolent intruders
On a rhythm deeper

Than we understood.
Was it the gaping world
That moved our blood

And made us coax our boats
For the last time into
A duel with the sea's wits

Until we lost sight of each known strand
And lay down to rest one night
On the thick mainland?

We hardly dare to ask the question
In this sluggish place.
Will we ever return

To where they stand
Upright, privileged, alone
And always threatened?

Since coming here we
Don't know whether our islands were
God washed by the human sea

Or our own selves under sun and cloud
Touched morning, noon and night
By the sea of God—

The kind of question asked by those
We live with,
Sophistic shadows

Severed from the sea's revealing shock,
From the summits' purity,
The tested rock.

The Dancer

Pity all other concern.
See the sun
Dance and burn

Through every room in the house.
How criminal we'd be
If we smothered in us

Our own dancing.
We would never know
How evening grows out of morning

And into morning again.
The dancer in the heart proclaims
Identity of love and pain

And is not troubled when the sky
Darkens with contradiction.
Though all night long the dancer dies

Fields breathe in the quickening east.
A human mimic, I resume
Defeat and conquest,

Knowing the dancer's lightness flows
Through the poplar and the grass,
The nettle and the rose.

Synge

His choice would be
The blue chasm of the waves,
The clean sea.

He'd roll through the waste
Forever
Finding the taste

Of weeds on his tongue
While in a small
White house among

The rocks, men and women
Kept glancing
At the door open to admit him
And his fiddle perfectly tuned.
He never came
And they went on dancing.

The Old Woman of Beare

(From the Irish.)

The sea crawls from the shore
Leaving there
The despicable weed,
A corpse's hair.
In me,
The desolate withdrawing sea.

The Old Woman of Beare am I
Who once was beautiful.
Now all I know is how to die.
I'll do it well.

Look at my skin
Stretched tight on the bone.
Where kings have pressed their lips,
The pain, the pain.

I don't hate the men
Who swore the truth was in their lies.
One thing alone I hate—
Women's eyes.

The young sun
Gives its youth to everyone,
Touching everything with gold.
In me, the cold.

The cold. Yet still a seed
Burns there.
Women love only money now.
But when
I loved, I loved
Young men.

Young men whose horses galloped
On many an open plain
Beating lightning from the ground.
I loved such men.

And still the sea
Rears and plunges into me,
Shoving, rolling through my head
Images of the drifting dead.

A soldier cries
Pitifully about his plight;
A king fades
Into the shivering night.

Does not every season prove
That the acorn hits the ground?
Have I not known enough of love
To know it's lost as soon as found?

I drank my fill of wine with kings,
Their eyes fixed on my hair.
Now among the stinking hags
I chew the cud of prayer.

Time was the sea
Brought kings as slaves to me.
Now I near the face of God
And the crab crawls through my blood.

I loved the wine
That thrilled me to my fingertips;
Now the spinster wind
Stitches salt into my lips.

The coward sea
Slouches away from me.
Fear brings back the tide
That made me stretch at the side
Of him who'd take me briefly for his bride.

The sea grows smaller, smaller now.
Farther, farther it goes
Leaving me here where the foam dries
On the deserted land,
Dry as my shrunken thighs,
As the tongue that presses my lips,
As the veins that break through my hands.

Cry

At the back of Bambury's field,
Rabbits play like children,
The curlew cries from the weed

That lies like lace on the shore,
Dressing the naked rocks and mud.
Grey gulls wheel and scatter

When the curlew cries. I hold my breath
When the curlew cries its frantic
Desolate words of love and death.

A curt ambassador, this; and bears
A pressing message, twisting its swift
Articulate body between the mud and stars.

It pleads and warns and is ignored,
Its lonely eloquence good proof
That in the beginning was the Word

Struck dumb between the mud and stars,
A lost cry in the heart of man,
A whimper sent between prison-bars

Of mad victory, sad defeat,
The hermit's prayer, the lover's vow,
The roisterer's shout in a late-night street,

Caught by the curlew in the Kerry sky,
Released like a curse or blessing
In the bleak injury of its cry.

Whatever it is, is clear to me,
Alone in a field of wonder
Where the Shannon twists to the sea.

The Shannon

Brown-legged girl and boy win seagrass
From the resolute rocks;
Their tiny figures move like birds
Beside the treacherous tranquillity of waves.
On this, the Kerry coast,
Peace hovers like an accusation
Over the unlaboured land;
Eloquent silence commemorates
The pointless scattering of love.
Between the Banner County and the Kingdom
The burly Shannon strides into the sea.
In rocky desolation, the unploughed parishes end;
The outnumbering waves insist
That the river is nobody's friend.